TRISTAN & ISOLDE

THE WARRIOR AND THE PRINCESS

A BRITISH LEGEND

**STORY BY
JEFF LIMKE**

**PENCILS AND INKS BY
RON RANDALL**

**ADAPTED FROM
CELTIC MYTHOLOGY
AND FROM
SIR THOMAS MALORY'S**
LE MORTE D'ARTHUR

ATLANTIC
OCEAN

IRELAND

TRISTAN & ISOLDE

THE WARRIOR AND THE PRINCESS

ENGLAND

A
BRITISH
LEGEND

IRISH
SEA

WALES

TINTAGEL

CORNWALL

ENGLISH CHANNEL

LERNER BOOKS LONDON • NEW YORK • MINNEAPOLIS

THE STORY OF TRISTAN AND ISOLDE DRAWS ON MANY INFLUENCES FROM THE ANCIENT CELTIC FOLKLORE AND MYTHOLOGY OF WALES, CORNWALL, AND BRITTANY. IN THE HIGH MIDDLE AGES (ABOUT A.D. 1100 TO 1300), THE LEGEND OF THEIR ROMANCE JOINED THE LARGE COLLECTION OF TALES ABOUT KING ARTHUR AND HIS KNIGHTS OF THE ROUND TABLE.

TRISTAN & ISOLDE'S THEME OF TWO YOUNG PEOPLE CAUGHT BETWEEN LOVE AND DUTY WAS COMMON IN MEDIEVAL ROMANCES. FEW PEOPLE IN THAT ERA MARRIED FOR LOVE. MOST MARRIAGES WERE ARRANGED BY PARENTS TO INCREASE A FAMILY'S WEALTH, STATUS, OR SECURITY. YOUNG PEOPLE UNDERSTOOD THEIR DUTY TO THEIR FAMILIES AND MOST NEVER EXPECTED TO BE ABLE TO CHOOSE THEIR OWN SPOUSES. YET THE THEME OF LOSING A TRUE LOVE AND BEING FORCED TO MARRY SOMEONE ELSE WAS POPULAR. IT REMAINED SO FOR CENTURIES, FEATURED IN WORKS RANGING FROM WILLIAM SHAKESPEARE'S SIXTEENTH-CENTURY PLAY *ROMEO AND JULIET* TO F. SCOTT FITZGERALD'S MODERN AMERICAN NOVEL *THE GREAT GATSBY*.

STORY BY JEFF LIMKE

PENCILS AND INKS BY RON RANDALL

COLOURING BY HI-FI DESIGN

LETTERING BY MARSHALL DILLON AND TERRI DELGADO

CONSULTANT: THERESA KRIER, PH.D., MACALESTER COLLEGE

Graphic Universe™ is a trademark of Lerner Publishing Group, Inc.

First published in the United Kingdom in 2010 by Lerner Books,
Dalton House,
60 Windsor Avenue,
London SW19 2RR

Website address: www.lernerbooks.co.uk

This edition edited for UK publication in 2010.

British Library Cataloguing in Publication Data

Limke, Jeff.
  Tristan & Isolde : the warrior and the princess.
  1. Tristan (Legendary character)—Comic books, strips, etc.—Juvenile fiction. 2. Iseult (Legendary character)—Comic books, strips, etc.—Juvenile fiction. 3. Children's stories—Comic books, strips, etc. I. Title
741.5-dc22

ISBN-13: 978 0 7613 5396 6

TABLE OF CONTENTS

TRISTAN THOUGHT IT WOULD BE A SIMPLE MISSION.

WEAK BUT STILL NOT OVERCOME BY THE SLOW-ACTING POISON, TRISTAN SAILED TO IRELAND. HE HAD TWO MISSIONS—TO BE CURED AND TO BRING BACK ISOLDE AS KING MARK'S BRIDE.

THAT WAS BEFORE HE CAME ACROSS THE DRAGON THAT RAVAGED THE IRISH COUNTRYSIDE.

AS THE STEWARD RODE OFF, THE REST OF THE PARTY DREW UP.

LET US BE SURE THE BEAST IS DEAD.

REMAIN THERE, MY LADIES, WHERE YOU ARE SAFE.

WAIT! THERE'S SOMETHING OVER THERE!

IT'S A MAN!

HE LIVES! HIS HEART BEATS. NOT VERY STRONGLY, BUT IT BEATS.

LIFT HIM ONTO HIS SHIELD.

CAREFUL. DON'T DROP HIM.

IF HE DEFEATED THE DRAGON, HE'S A HERO, MOTHER.

WE MUST GET HIM TO THE CASTLE. I WILL CURE HIS ILLS.

TRISTAN SET SAIL FROM IRELAND WITH PRINCESS ISOLDE AND BRENGWAINE.

THE SEAS WERE ROUGH, AND ISOLDE BECAME SEASICK.

RENGWAINE, I KNOW YOU PACKED A LITTLE WINE. FETCH SOME, PLEASE.

I THINK IT WILL HELP SETTLE THE PRINCESS'S STOMACH.

YES, I'LL GET IT RIGHT AWAY.

WORRIED ABOUT ISOLDE, BRENGWAINE DIDN'T LOOK CLOSELY AT THE WINE SACK SHE CHOSE. SHE DIDN'T REALIZE—

—THAT IT WAS NOT WINE.

MAY I HAVE A BIT? MY STOMACH IS A BIT UPSET TOO.

IT WAS THE LOVE POTION.

A WEDDING IN CORNWALL

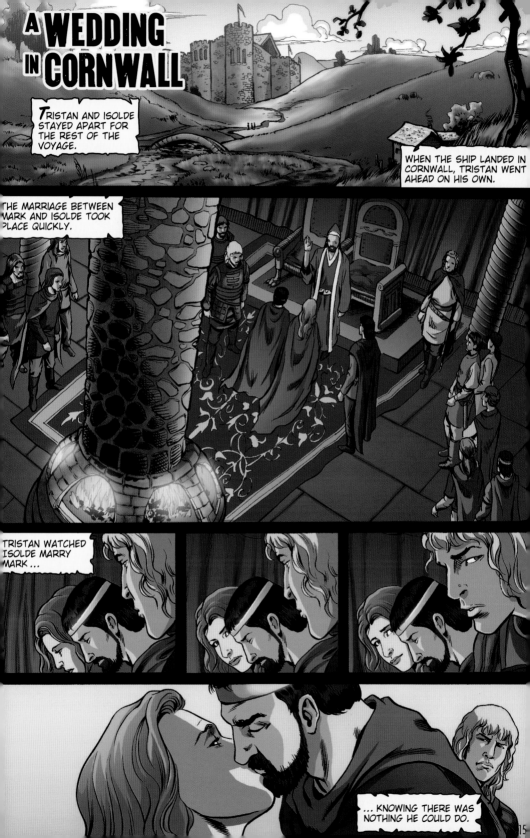

TRISTAN AND ISOLDE STAYED APART FOR THE REST OF THE VOYAGE.

WHEN THE SHIP LANDED IN CORNWALL, TRISTAN WENT AHEAD ON HIS OWN.

THE MARRIAGE BETWEEN MARK AND ISOLDE TOOK PLACE QUICKLY.

TRISTAN WATCHED ISOLDE MARRY MARK ...

... KNOWING THERE WAS NOTHING HE COULD DO.

15

MARK TRIED TO BE A KIND HUSBAND. BUT HIS DUTIES KEPT HIM VERY BUSY. ISOLDE TURNED TO TRISTAN FOR COMPANIONSHIP.

IT IS WRONG THAT TRISTAN AND THE QUEEN SPEND SO MUCH TIME TOGETHER, LLUD.

THEY ARE ONLY TALKING, AND THEY ARE IN PUBLIC, SIR MERIADOC.

I DO NOT TRUST THOSE TWO

MUST I LISTEN AGAIN TO HOW YOU ARE SURE HE AND QUEEN ISOLDE MEET IN SECRET?

I AM SORRY, MY KING, BUT IT IS UNWISE TO LEAVE THEM ALONE.

EXCUSE ME BUT PERHA I HAVE A SOLUTION

LET SIR MERIADOC PROTECT TH QUEEN RATHE THAN SIR TRISTAN.

BRENGWAINE— A WONDERFUL SOLUTION.

DO YOU HEAR, MERIADOC? I PLACE QUEEN ISOLDE UNDER YOUR CARE.

"YES, KING MARK. IN FACT, I WILL CHECK ON THE QUEEN RIGHT NOW."

MY LADY, YOU MUST GET HIM OUT!

SIR MERIADOC IS ON HIS WAY UP HERE!

MERIADOC WILL TELL KING MARK THAT HE FOUND YOU TOGETHER. IT WILL LOOK VERY BAD.

GO, SIR KNIGHT! TAKE THE BACK STAIRWAY!

RRRIP

YOU SHALL BE THE DEATH OF ME YET, YOUNG LADY.

NOW HURRY! LOOK AS IF NOTHING IS AMISS.

IS YOUR MAJESTY ALL RIGHT? I HEARD QUITE A RACKET.

YOU WERE ALONE THE WHOLE TIME, WERE YOU?

THEN WOULD YOU CARE TO EXPLAIN THIS?

YES, I'M FINE. BRENGWAINE JUST RETURNED FROM DOWNSTAIRS.

I THOUGHT NOT.

MERIADOC WASTED NO TIME TELLING KING MARK.

... IS TORN FROM SIR TRISTAN'S CLOAK.

THIS EVIDENCE SHOWS HE HAS BETRAYED YOU, MY KING. WE AWAIT YOUR JUDGMENT.

THIS JUDGMENT IS NOT EASY FOR ME.

MERIADOC, I PUT MY WIFE IN YOUR CARE, AND YOU HAVE DONE ALL THAT I HAVE ASKED.

TRISTAN, YOU ARE MY NEPHEW AND MY BEST KNIGHT.

MY QUEEN, I KNOW I HAVE NEGLECTED YOU BECAUSE OF MY DUTIES.

BUT TRISTAN AND ISOLDE, YOU HAVE BOTH ACTED DISHONORABLY.

TRISTAN, YOU ARE BANISHED. YOU WILL LEAVE MY KINGDOM AT ONCE.

IF YOU RETURN, YOUR PUNISHMENT WILL BE DEATH.

AS YOU SAY, MY LIEGE.

ISOLDE WAITED FOR TRISTAN, NOT KNOWING THAT MERIADOC HAD SET A TRAP.

EVEN AFTER BEING BANISHED, TRISTAN HAD COME TO THIS TREE EVERY DAY. FOR MONTHS HE WAITED FOR ISOLDE TO FIND ONE OF HIS SECRET MESSAGES.

NOW THEY WOULD FINALLY MEET AGAIN.

HIS HEART BEAT FASTER AS HE LOOKED UPON HER FACE. SHE WAS BEAUTIFUL TO HIM EVEN FROM A DISTANCE.

THEN TRISTAN SAW THE SHADOW OF A MAN IN THE TREE ABOVE ISOLDE. HIS HEART FELL.

HE KNEW SIR MERIADOC WAS BEHIND THIS TRAP.

HE WOULD HAVE TO TRY TO MEET ISOLDE SOMEWHERE ELSE, ON ANOTHER DAY.

YOUR DESTINY IS GUARDED BY ANGELS, ISOLDE. SO I GRANT YOU ONE MORE CHANCE.

HAVE YOU BEEN UNFAITHFUL TO ME?

MY KING, I CAN TRUTHFULLY SAY NO MAN OTHER THAN THIS PEASANT HAS EVER TOUCHED ME.

AND IF HE HADN'T TOUCHED ME, I WOULD HAVE DIED.

GUARDS, RELEASE THE PEASANT.

AND PEASANT, NEVER LET ME SEE YOU AGAIN.

WITH THAT, TRISTAN LEFT CORNWALL, KING MARK, AND HIS LOVE, ISOLDE.

25

KING MARK WANTED TO BELIEVE HIS WIFE. HE WANTED THEIRS TO BE A HAPPY MARRIAGE.

BUT HE COULD NOT IGNORE SIR MERIADOC'S EVIDENCE.

FOR HER PART, ISOLDE WAITED ONLY FOR TRISTAN TO COME BACK FOR HER. HE SECRETLY SENT GIFTS, INCLUDING A DOG NAMED PETTIGRUE.

BUT TRISTAN DID NOT RETURN. HE HAD LEFT TO FIGHT AS A KNIGHT FOR OTHER KINGS.

HE FORGAVE TRISTAN AND WELCOMED HIM BACK.

IN TIME, KING MARK'S HEART SOFTENED. TRISTAN HAD BEEN HIS BEST KNIGHT, AND KING MARK NEEDED HIM TO PROTECT HIS PEOPLE.

TRISTAN RETURNS

TOGETHER, MARK AND TRISTAN FOUGHT BATTLES.

TRISTAN ALSO SPENT TIME WITH ISOLDE. HE ENTERTAINED HER WITH SONGS OF HEROISM AND ROMANCE.

AND ISOLDE WATCHED FROM AFAR AS TRISTAN PRACTICED HIS SKILLS AS A KNIGHT.

SIR MERIADOC CONTINUED TO SPY ON THE TWO. HE WAS SURE THEY WERE BETRAYING THE KING.

THOUGH HE HAD NO EVIDENCE, MERIADOC SPREAD HIS GOSSIP.

THE UGLY RUMOURS WORKED ON KING MARK.

I HAVE BEEN VERY PATIENT WITH YOU, BUT YOU HAVE BETRAYED ME YET AGAIN.

YOU BOTH WILL LEAVE THIS COURT UNTIL I COMMAND YOU TO RETURN.

27

TRISTAN AND ISOLDE TRIED TO BE FAITHFUL TO THE KING. THEY STAYED AWAY FROM EACH OTHER AND DID NOT COMMUNICATE.

BUT TRUE LOVERS COULD NOT BE KEPT APART FOR LONG.

TRISTAN AND ISOLDE WERE OVERJOYED JUST TO SEE EACH OTHER. ALONE IN THE CAVE, THEY THOUGHT NO ONE WOULD LEARN OF THEIR MEETING.

THEY SHOULD HAVE KNOWN BETTER.

KNIGHT-ERRANT

OVER TIME, MARK AND ISOLDE HEARD NEWS OF TRISTAN.

THEY HEARD OF HIS SLAYING THREE GIANTS IN SPAIN...

... OF HIS FIGHTING IN BRITTANY FOR THE DUKE OF FLORENCE...

... AND OF HIS MARRIAGE TO ANOTHER ISOLDE, ISOLDE OF THE WHITE HAND.

IN HIS SADNESS, HE SHUT HIMSELF AWAY FROM HIS WIFE.

AFTER HIS WEDDING, TRISTAN OCCUPIED HIMSELF WITH BUILDING HIS OWN CASTLE.

BY CHOICE, HE KNEW LITTLE OF WHAT OCCURRED IN TINTAGEL.

HE HAD MARRIED HER TO FORGET HIS ISOLDE.

IT HADN'T WORKED. HE COULD NOT FORGET HIS FIRST LOVE.

IS SHE NOT BEAUTIFUL, GANHARD?

YES, TRISTAN, SHE IS. BUT YOU ARE MARRIED NOW. YOU MUST BE KINDER TO MY SISTER, YOUR WIFE. SHE PINES FOR YOU AS YOU PINE FOR THIS ISOLDE.

THIS SCULPTURE COMES NOWHERE NEAR CATCHING ISOLDE'S BEAUTY.

I UNDERSTAND.

NO, YOU DON'T. SHE IS MY TRUE LOVE. MY ONLY LOVE.

SIR TRISTAN, I BEAR NEWS FROM KING MARK. HIS CASTLE IS UNDER SIEGE. HE ASKS FOR YOUR AID.

ISOLDE OF THE WHITE HAND WAS WAITING WHEN GANHARD BROUGHT THE WOUNDED TRISTAN.

MY HUSBAND, WE NEED TO BLEED YOUR INFECTION.

YOU WILL NOT HEAL IF WE DON'T.

NO ... IT DOES ... NOT ... WORK.

PLEASE ... SEND THE DOCTOR ... AWAY.

BUT MY HUSBAND—

PLEASE.

GANHARD. I ... NEED TO TALK ... TO YOU.

YOU ARE MY ... CLOSEST ... FRIEND.

TAKE THIS TO ... ISOLDE IN ... CORNWALL. GIVE THIS RING ... TO ... HER.

ASK HER TO COME TO ME.

ONLY SHE CAN ... SAVE ME.

SIR GANHARD LEFT FOR CORNWALL AS SOON AS HE COULD.

HE KNEW HE HAD LITTLE TIME.

ISOLDE GRIEVED TO HEAR THAT TRISTAN'S WOUND HAD NOT HEALED. SHE KNEW WHAT SHE HAD TO DO.

IN LESS THAN AN HOUR, GANHARD, QUEEN ISOLDE, AND BRENGWAINE WERE READY AND RIDING.

THE WIND HAD BEEN FAVOURABLE, AND THE SHIP RETURNED FASTER THAN GANHARD HAD HOPED.

OH MY!

WHAT ... IS IT? WHAT DO YOU ... SEE?

A SHIP SAILS UP THE RIVER.

TRISTAN'S WIFE, JEALOUS OF HIS LOVE OF ISOLDE, DID NOT ANSWER TRUTHFULLY.

IT FLIES A BLACK SAIL.

I WONDER WHAT THAT MEANS?

A SHIP? WHAT ... WHAT COLOUR IS ITS SAIL?

NOTHING.

IT MEANS NOTHING AT—

WHAT, MY HUSBAND?

SPEAK TO ME AGAIN. WHAT DID YOU SAY?

NOOOOOOOO! WHAT HAVE I DONE?

YOU CANNOT DIE!

GANHARD DID AS HE PROMISED. KING MARK HEARD THE TALE OF THE LOVE POTION. AND HE FINALLY UNDERSTOOD TRISTAN AND ISOLDE'S GRIEF AT BEING SEPARATED.

ISOLDE WAS HIS WIFE, BUT MARK KNEW HE HAD NOT LOVED HER AS TRISTAN HAD.

MARK NO LONGER WANTED TO STAND IN THE WAY OF SUCH A POWERFUL LOVE.

HE HAD KEPT TRISTAN AND ISOLDE APART IN LIFE.

NOW THE KING WOULD DO WHAT HE COULD TO MAKE UP FOR THAT.

HE LET THEM BE TOGETHER FOR ETERNITY BENEATH A PILLAR OF STONE FOR ALL TO SEE.

GLOSSARY

ANGUIN: an Irish king and Isolde's father

BRENGWAINE: Isolde's lady-in-waiting

CORNWALL: a county on the south western tip of England. Until the early Middle Ages, Cornwall was ruled by chieftains and minor kings.

COURT: the place from which a sovereign (such as a king) rules. The term also refers to the family, advisers, and friends of the king who attend him at court.

ERRANT: wandering or travelling. A knight-errant was a knight who traveled from place to place looking for adventures or offering his services as a soldier.

ISEULT: an Irish queen and the mother of Isolde

ISOLDE: an Irish princess and the wife of King Mark of Cornwall

KNIGHT: a mounted soldier sworn to loyally serve a lord or ruler. In the Middle Ages, when a man became a knight, he swore an oath. He promised to obey religious law, defend the weak, honour women, serve his king and protect his country.

LADY-IN-WAITING: a woman who serves a queen or a princess

LORD: a ruler or landowner with authority over a group of people

MERIADOC: a knight in King Mark's court

PEASANT: a person of low birth

SECOND: a person who assists another during a duel or a fight

SIEGE: a military attack on a castle or fort, to force the occupants to surrender

STEWARD: a servant in a castle or a large house. Stewards usually had a high rank among the servants.

TINTAGEL: King Mark's castle. Tintagel is a real castle on the north coast of Cornwall, England. It has been linked to Arthurian legend since the twelfth century A.D.

TREASON: the crime of betraying a sovereign (such as a king), which is seen as endangering the order and the safety of the kingdom

TRISTAN: a knight and the nephew of King Mark

WINE SACK: a pouch, often made of animal skin, with a top that closed, made for carrying wine

FURTHER READING AND WEBSITES

Ash, Geoffery. *The Discovery of King Arthur*. London: The History Press Ltd, 2005. Geoffrey Ash, an Arthurian expert sets out to determine once and for all if King Arthur really existed.

Miles, Rosalind. *Isolde: Queen of the Western Isle*. New York: Crown Publishers Ltd, 2002. The first of the Tristan and Isolde novels in hardback.

Crossley-Holland, Kevin. *The World of King Arthur and His Court: People, Places, Legend and Lore*. New York: Dutton Books, 2004. An illustrated guide providing information on key characters, daily life in a castle, knighthood, and other aspects of Arthurian legend.

Snyder, Christopher. *Exploring the World of King Arthur*. London: Thames & Hudson Ltd, 2000. A survey of, and companion to, all things connected with the Arthurian legend.

Tristan & Isolde. DVD. Los Angeles: 20th Century Fox Home Entertainment, 2006.

King Arthur
http://tlc.discovery.com/convergence/arthur/arthur.html
The Learning Channel's website features a gallery of Arthurian images, an interactive section on the legend of Arthur, and a timeline of Britain in the Dark Ages.

King Arthur and the Knights of the Round Table
http://www.kingarthursknights.com
This website provides articles on the historical and legendary Arthur, a map and information on Arthurian sites, artwork, and the stories of the knights and other characters of the famous legend.

CREATING *TRISTAN & ISOLDE*

In creating this story, author Jeff Limke used Thomas Malory's *Le Morte d'Arthur* and *Popular Romances of the Middle Ages* by George Cox and Eustace Jones. Artist Ron Randall used many historical and traditional sources to shape the story's visual details. Consultant Theresa Krier used her knowledge of Arthurian lore and medieval culture to ensure accuracy.

original pencil sketch from page 31

INDEX

ABOUT THE AUTHOR AND THE ARTIST

JEFF LIMKE was raised in North Dakota, where he first read, listened to, and marveled at Arthurian tales of knights and their adventures. Limke later taught these stories for many years and has written several adaptations of them. His Graphic Myths and Legends work includes *King Arthur: Excalibur Unsheathed*, *Isis & Osiris: To the Ends of the Earth*, *Thor & Loki: In the Land of Giants*, *Jason: Quest for the Golden Fleece*, *Theseus: Battling the Minotaur*, and *Arthur & Lancelot: The Fight for Camelot*. Other stories have been published by Caliber Comics, Arrow Comics, and Kenzer and Company.

RON RANDALL has drawn comics for every major comic book publisher in the United States, including Marvel, DC, Image, and Dark Horse. His Graphic Myths and Legends work includes *Thor & Loki: In the Land of Giants*, *Amaterasu: Return of the Sun*, *Beowulf: Monster Slayer*, and *Guan Yu: Blood Brothers to the End*. He has also worked on superhero comics such as Justice League and Spiderman; science fiction titles such as *Star Wars* and *Star Trek*; fantasy adventure titles such as *DragonLance* and *Warlord*; suspense and horror titles including *SwampThing*, *Predator*, and *Venom*; and his own creation, *Trekker*.

First published in the United States of America in 2008